FOREWORD

The carefully written partbooks of Robert Dow, one of the manuscript sources of   s,
contain the following colophon to this piece:

> Non ita mœsta sonant plangentis verba prophetæ
> Quam sonat authoris musica mœsta mei.

An attempt to put this tribute into English, capturing something of the flavor of its alliteration and hexameter rhythms, might be:

> Móurnful to mé thèse wórds of the plángènt próphet of óld tìmes
> Yét mòre móurnful this músic now sóundìng fórth from its mákèr.

Such a eulogy in respect of White's five-part Lamentations is hard to better. Whoever the prophet was (the ancient ascription to Jeremiah does not stand up) his stark poetry is well matched by the Latin translation and the English of the King James Version. Its dejection is movingly echoed in music which wonderfully portrays the bitter catastrophe of the Babylonian captivity. White sometimes employs blocks of harmony, at others sustained polyphony, but always making the most understated of gestures. This is why these Lamentations (whose particular selection of verses is unique to White) stand out as having been more movingly rendered than those by any other composer—including White himself in his six-part setting of the same non-liturgical text, which must have had some particular significance for him.

The Lamentations of composers such as Tallis and Byrd are certainly very fine, but White eschews their dramatic gestures (and indeed their scoring), and with a palette of voices that he could have employed even more colorfully than theirs, chooses instead to reflect the weary bleakness of the prophet's austere message. The traditional refrain ('Jerusalem, convertere . . . ') added to each group of verses is one striking instance among many: White's reflection of the prophet's plea for conversion is not full of rhetoric; instead, it is redolent of the desolation and near-hopelessness of the devastation portrayed by the prophet. For my part (we recorded most of the English settings of the Lamentations over the years) I cannot recall being more moved by such 'mournful music' as by this. Curiously, what appears to be the Hebrew word for 'acrostic', the reason for the original initial letters of each verse being sung in the Latin version, is derived from the root 'spell', in both senses of the word. Truly, this grief-stricken music is spellbinding.

DAVID WULSTAN, 2009

David Wulstan conducted the Clerkes of Oxenford in White's five-part Lamentations for Calliope (1976), a recording that was subsequently reissued many times, both on the Calliope and Nonesuch labels.

PREFACE

Maxima musarum nostrarum gloria White   White, thou glorious leader of our art hast died
Tu peris aeternum sed tua musa manet.   But thy muse lives on in eternity.

[from the partbooks copied by Robert Dow in the early 1580s]

Like his contemporary Robert Parsons, Robert White's life was cut short by misfortune; he and his family fell victim to a virulent outbreak of plague in the Westminster area of London in 1574. Born in the 1530s (scholarly opinions about the date vary between 1530–32 and *c*.1538), his years of maturity as a composer coincided with the early part of Elizabeth I's reign, and he took up the prestigious post of Master of the Choristers at Westminster Abbey in 1569. He had spent the years 1555–62 at Trinity College, Cambridge, then succeeded Christopher Tye (his father-in-law) as Master of the Choristers at Ely Cathedral, moving on to Chester Cathedral in 1566. Apart from some works for instrumental consort, the main part of his surviving output consists of Latin sacred music: a number of psalm motets, hymns, and two Lamentations.

The Lamentations belong to a tradition whose origins are found in the Lessons drawn from the biblical Lamentations of Jeremiah that were heard during the Holy Week offices of the Catholic church. From the 16th century onwards composers began to set these Lessons to polyphonic music, both in mainland Europe and, a little later, in Elizabethan England. The circumstances in which a number of English composers came to write them are curiously unclear, however, because unlike the settings by Palestrina and Lassus, they do not fit into the liturgy as prescribed at the time of their composition. The accession of the Protestant Elizabeth I in 1558 was soon followed by a religious settlement that included limitation of the use of Latin-texted service music to the Chapel Royal and the universities of Oxford and Cambridge, places where it would have been understood. It is clear that Latin polyphony continued to be composed in the 1560s and 70s, and that some time later in the reign three collector-copyists valued it so highly that they each compiled retrospective anthologies of it: John Sadler, Robert Dow, and John Baldwin (see Editorial Notes for details), each of whom included some Lamentations in their sets of partbooks, thereby ensuring the music's survival for posterity.

The composers—Parsley, Byrd, White, Tallis, and Alfonso Ferrabosco—must have been attracted to these melancholy texts not only for their potential to elicit an expressive musical response, but also, if they had Catholic sympathies, for the particular significance of the texts for their own times. Whether the music was originally intended for liturgical use, or devotional or recreational use in a domestic context, is difficult to establish with certainty, but the imagery of Jerusalem and its destruction had well-known layers of metaphorical association with 'Rome' and the Catholic church, increasingly under threat in England at this time.

In our own times, the popularity (and availability in modern editions) of Tallis's Lamentations is such that it has tended to overshadow the settings by his English contemporaries, which deserve to be more widely known and performed; in particular, Robert White's five-part Lamentations can surely be regarded as one of the composer's finest works. Though the particular selection of verses that White chose (*Lamentations* I, vv.8–13) does not appear to tally with any recognised Lesson, he made two settings of it, respectively for five and six voices. They share the distinctive Phrygian mode as well as a few brief melodic resemblances, but in other respects present very different musical approaches. The five-part setting is the more forward-looking of the two, its music moving between expressive contrapuntal writing and block chords where one voice leads the others; in the course of this lengthy and impassioned text White introduces some remarkably bold harmonic shifts and reveals an exceptional depth of emotion. The music's structure is governed by that of the text, where each verse is prefaced by a Hebrew letter, presented in alphabetical sequence. These letters afforded the composer an opportunity to show his skill in writing abstract music, their decoration perhaps comparable to that practised by

OXFORD

SSATB choir, unaccompanied

Robert White

Lamentations (a5)

V- fica Dei donum optimi

trahit, trahit homines trahit, trahit homines, tra- hit Deos, trahit

Deos, Mu- fica, musica, Mu- fi-

Series Editors: Sally Dunkley & Francis Steele

MUSICA DEI DONUM

MUSICA DEI DONUM

The series MUSICA DEI DONUM sets out to make accessible to performers a variety of interesting and generally less well-known vocal works. They are presented in practical format, with the aim of retaining a 'clean' text on the page; at the same time we have offered some performance suggestions for those who wish to consider them, placed in the vocal reduction. Whilst the reduction can be played on a keyboard, our priority has been to preserve the integrity of the vocal lines rather than to present an idiomatically pianistic score.

These editions have been prepared from original sources, brief details of which are provided, but this material is selective rather than comprehensive in scope. We prefer instead to offer something of real value to the performer: introductory comments which give an overview, surveying the piece from the vantage point of personal experience of the music in performance, and translations (commissioned especially for this series from Jeremy White) which aim to enable the performer to bring musical and verbal text into the same focal plane.

SALLY DUNKLEY & FRANCIS STEELE, 2007

EDITOR BIOGRAPHIES

Sally Dunkley's interest in 16th-century vocal music was established during her years as a student at Oxford University, where she sang with the pioneering group the Clerkes of Oxenford and studied with its director, David Wulstan. Since then, her career as a professional consort singer has developed hand-in-hand with continuing in-depth study of the music as editor, writer, researcher, and teacher. The experience of working with several of the leading British groups in this area—she is a founder member of The Sixteen and sang over 1000 concerts with The Tallis Scholars—has afforded her unique insights into questions of performance practice. She has been involved in the preparation of practical scholarly editions over several decades and is increasingly engaged in sharing her experience through workshops and summer schools.

Francis Steele was born in Liverpool, the son of a docker. Christ's Hospital school nurtured his early musical interests, and while at Magdalen College, Oxford, he studied with David Wulstan and Dr. Bernard Rose, two remarkable mentors who combined scholarship with performance. This influence pervaded a singing career spanning nearly three decades, during which Francis sang with and furnished editions for the foremost British ensembles. Traveling and performing extensively, he has developed an intimate practical knowledge of Renaissance repertoire, and his main concern is an imaginative fidelity to musical and verbal text. Francis now lives at *La Maison Verte* in southern France, where he runs courses advocating this approach; he also coaches groups throughout Europe and in the USA.

medieval scribes illuminating initial capitals. The verses of the Lamentations culminate with the exhortation 'Jerusalem, Jerusalem, convertere ad Dominum Deum tuum' ('Jerusalem, Jerusalem, return again to the Lord your God') which in White's setting is heard twice, at the halfway point as well as at the conclusion.

Like so much Tudor church music, the Lamentations are known to have been performed early in the 20th century at Westminster Cathedral, London, under the direction of that great advocate and pioneer R. R. Terry.[1] More recent interest in them began to be shown in the recordings made by Scuola di Chiesa, conductor John Hoban (1968), and the Clerkes of Oxenford, conductor David Wulstan (1976). An edition by David Mateer was published in the *Early English Church Music* series (vol.xxxii) in 1986.

SALLY DUNKLEY, 2009

[1] Timothy Day, 'Sir Richard Terry and 16th-century polyphony', *Early Music,* xxii (1994), p.298

TEXT AND TRANSLATION

Heth

Peccatum peccavit Jerusalem,
propterea instabilis facta est.
Omnes qui glorificabant eam
spreverunt illam,
quia viderunt ignominiam eius;
ipsa autem gemens
et conversa est retrorsum.

Jerusalem has committed a great sin,
and therefore she has become untrustworthy.
All who used to praise her
have spurned her,
because they have seen her shame;
and she groans
and has turned away her face.

Teth

Sordes eius in pedibus eius,
nec recordata est finis sui.
Deposita est vehementer,
non habens consolatorem.
Vide, Domine, afflictionem meam,
quoniam erectus est inimicus.

Her own filth is upon her feet,
and she has given no thought to her purpose.
She has been brought very low,
and has none to comfort her.
'Look, Lord, upon my suffering,
and see how my enemy is exalted.'

Iod

Manum suam misit hostis
ad omnia desiderabilia eius,
quia vidit gentes
ingressas sanctuarium suum
de quibus preceperas
ne intrarent in ecclesiam tuam.

The foe has laid hands
on all that was dear to her,
for she has seen the foreigner
enter her sanctuary,
the men you decreed
should never be admitted into your assembly.

Jerusalem, Jerusalem,
convertere ad Dominum Deum tuum.

Jerusalem, Jerusalem,
return again to the Lord your God.

Caph

Omnis populus eius gemens
et quaerens panem;
dederunt preciosa quaeque pro cibo
ad refocillandam animam.
Vide, Domine, et considera
quoniam facta sum vilis.

All her people are groaning
as they search for bread;
they have given anything of value for food
to keep themselves alive.
'Look, Lord, and mark
how low I have sunk.'

Lamed

O vos omnes qui transitis per viam,
attendite et videte
si est dolor sicut dolor meus,
quoniam vindemiavit me,
ut locutus est Dominus
in die irae furoris sui.

'All you who pass by on the road,
stop and see
if there be any grief like my grief,
for the Lord has pressed me like the grape,
as he said he would
on the day of his furious rage.'

Mem

De excelso misit ignem
in ossibus meis, et erudivit me;
expandit rete pedibus meis,
convertit me retrorsum.
Posuit me desolationem,
tota die maerore confectam.

'From on high he has sent a fire
into my very bones, and has taught me;
he has spread a net to snare my feet,
and has reversed my course.
He has left me abandoned,
exhausted from mourning all day long.'

Jerusalem, Jerusalem,
convertere ad Dominum Deum tuum.

Jerusalem, Jerusalem,
return again to the Lord your God.

JEREMY WHITE, TRANS.

PERFORMANCE NOTES

Like so much English polyphony of this period, White's five-part Lamentations may best be performed with a real understanding of the text and the music: its rhetoric, phrase structure and harmonic progressions. Expressive phrasing generated from the harmonic impetus is of the essence in communicating the power of this music to the listener, while too much 'interpretation' may not serve it so well. In particular, extreme dynamics are best avoided as they may disturb its essentially contemplative nature. The performance suggestions shown in the vocal reduction of this edition naturally reflect our personal view of the music, which was initially shaped by the experience of singing it under the direction of David Wulstan. We have endeavored to make them reflect something of his articulation of the work's desolation (see Foreword), though there are of course other different and equally valid interpretations, which might be more dramatically engaged and extrovert, for example.

The choice of tempi will naturally depend on the size of ensemble and the acoustic of the building. However, there is a policy decision to be made, whether to take the Hebrew letters at the same speed as the verses, or at a slower speed. In several of the other Elizabethan Lamentations, such as those of Byrd, the six-voice ones of White, and some parts of Tallis's settings, the harmonic movement of the music of the letters suggests that a slower speed is appropriate, but for the five-voice Lamentations of White the music is not so determining—either way is possible and can sound convincing.

This edition presents the music transposed up a tone. The vocal range of the 'alto' part, as so often at this time, is unusually wide-ranging, and it may be helpful to have a tenor or two to double the lowest notes, and perhaps an alto to double the lowest phrases of soprano 2 as well.

It should be emphasized that in this edition all accidentals, whether on the stave or above it, apply up to the end of the bar, according to normal convention; the addition of cautionary accidentals has been limited as far as possible, though given the music's unusual harmonic scope, many more could have been printed. Two forms of the same pitch (natural and sharp, etc.) often appear in immediate juxtaposition (e.g. mm.46–7), as a characteristic element of the composer's style.

Depending on the tempi adopted, the duration of White's five-part Lamentations in performance is likely to be around 20 minutes or more, and the question may therefore arise, especially bearing in mind the interim 'Jerusalem, convertere' refrain (mm.175–197), whether or not this was intended as one single piece of music. Unlike the Lamentations of Tallis, clearly two separate works for different occasions, there is no evidence to suggest that White's setting was other than a single work, and at least one copyist (Robert Dow) viewed it as a two-section piece (like many of the *Cantiones sacrae* of Byrd, for example), advising the singer to turn the page for the second part ('Caph', m.198), a division that implies no more than a double bar-line in modern notation. It may be significant that in his six-part Lamentations White set exactly the same portion of text, the only structural difference being that there is no intermediate refrain, and so no reason for us to think of questioning that the work is other than a single entity. In practical terms, however, the possibility of performing one or other half of the five-part setting may be worth considering.

SALLY DUNKLEY, 2009

Lamentations (a5)

ROBERT WHITE (*c*.1538–74)
ed. Sally Dunkley

Sally Dunkley has asserted her right under the United Kingdom Copyright, Designs, and Patents Act, 1988, to be identified as the Editor of this work.

2

Peccátum peccávit Jerúsalem,
Jerusalem has committed a great sin,

quia vidérunt ignomíniam éius;
because they have seen her shame;

Sórdes éius in pédibus éius,
Her own filth is upon her feet,

meandering, as if distraught [♩ = 85]

nec recordáta est fínis súi.
and she has given no thought to her purpose.

Depósita est veheménter,
She has been brought very low,

10

quóniam eréctus est inimícus.
and see how my enemy is exalted.'

12

Mánum súam mísit hóstis
The foe has laid hands

ne intrárent in ecclésiam túam.
should never be admitted into your assembly.

18

Jerúsalem, Jerúsalem, convértere ad Dóminum Déum túum.
Jerusalem, Jerusalem, return again to the Lord your God.

22

Víde, Dómine, et consídera
'Look, Lord, and mark

si est dólor sícut dólor méus,
if there be any grief like my grief,

29

De excélso mísit ígnem
'From on high he has sent a fire

becoming calm

vigorous, controlled energy [♩ = 80]

Jerúsalem, Jerúsalem, convértere ad Dóminum Déum túum.
Jerusalem, Jerusalem, return again to the Lord your God.

EDITORIAL NOTES

Text
Lamentations I, vv.8–13

Sources
The main sources consulted for this edition are:
Oxford, Bodleian Library, Mss.Mus.e.1–5, f.40
Oxford, Christ Church Library, Mss.979–83, no.33 (lacking tenor)
Oxford, Christ Church Library, Mss.984–88, no.1

The Lamentations, or excerpts from them, are also found in a number of other incomplete sources, including several from the Paston group.[1]

Because of the length of the work, the large number of manuscript sources and the exceptional number of accidentals in the music, the full critical commentary listing all the variants between sources is very substantial, and printing it lies outside the remit of this performing edition. It may be consulted in *Early English Church Music*, vol.xxxii (ed. David Mateer), where it extends over six pages of densely abbreviated symbols. Whilst there are many alternative readings of the word underlay, with consequent minor rhythmic variants, we can be reasonably confident about the music itself, not least because the wide-ranging nature of its harmonic vocabulary required that an unusually large number of accidentals be specified, leaving less scope for doubt than in many works of its time.

This edition is based primarily on the set of partbooks from the Bodleian Library, Mss.Mus.e.1–5, copied by John Sadler (1513–after 1591) during the 1570s and early 80s.[2] White's music is well represented in this source, along with that of Taverner, Tallis, Byrd, and other composers of Latin-texted music, a choice that may reflect some sympathy with the Catholic cause. David Mateer's study of the compilation of these partbooks suggests that White's Lamentations had probably been copied by about 1570, and they immediately follow the two settings by Tallis. In another source, the partbooks that Robert Dow began to assemble in 1581 (Oxford, Christ Church Library, Mss.984–8),[3] White's music is given pride of place at the very beginning, with the Lamentations standing at the head of eight of the composer's works. This, together with the affectionate couplets (see Foreword and Preface), seem to suggest that composer and scribe may have been acquainted. The third source, copied by John Baldwin (Oxford, Christ Church Library, Mss.979–83),[4] is thought to date from the 1590s.

Pitch, note values
The music has been transposed up a tone in this edition, and the note values halved.

I should like to thank the Bodleian Library, Oxford, and the Governing Body of Christ Church, Oxford, for permission to publish this edition based on transcriptions from manuscripts in their collections.

SALLY DUNKLEY, 2009

[1] Philip Brett, 'Edward Paston (1550–1630): a Norfolk Gentleman and his musical collection', *Transactions of the Cambridge Bibliographical Society*, iv (1964), pp.51–69

[2] David Mateer, 'John Sadler and Oxford, Bodleian Mss. Mus.e.1–5', *Music & Letters*, lx (1979), pp.281–95

[3] David Mateer, 'Oxford, Christ Church Music Mss.984–88: an index and commentary', *RMA Research Chronicle*, xx (1986), pp.1–18

[4] Roger Bray, 'The part-books Oxford, Christ Church, Mss.979–83: an index and commentary', *Musica Disciplina*, xxv (1971), pp.179–97, and 'John Baldwin', *Music & Letters*, lvi (1975), pp.55–9

MUSICA DEI DONUM is a new early-music series that features a variety of lesser-known, interesting, and accessible works edited by early-music experts Sally Dunkley and Francis Steele. These editions have been prepared from original sources and are presented in a practical, uncluttered format. Performance suggestions appear in the vocal reduction, and running translations, commissioned especially for this series from Jeremy White, are positioned above each system for the edification and convenience of the performer.

Also from the MUSICA DEI DONUM series

Cipriano de Rore—Descendi in hortum meum

Orlandus Lassus—Musica, Dei donum optimi

Philippe de Monte and William Byrd—Super flumina Babylonis and Quomodo cantabimus

William Mundy—Beatus et sanctus and Sive vigilem

John Sheppard—Missa Cantate

V- fica Dei donum optimi

OXFORD

UNIVERSITY PRESS

www.oup.com

ISBN 978-0-19-380491-3

9 780193 804913